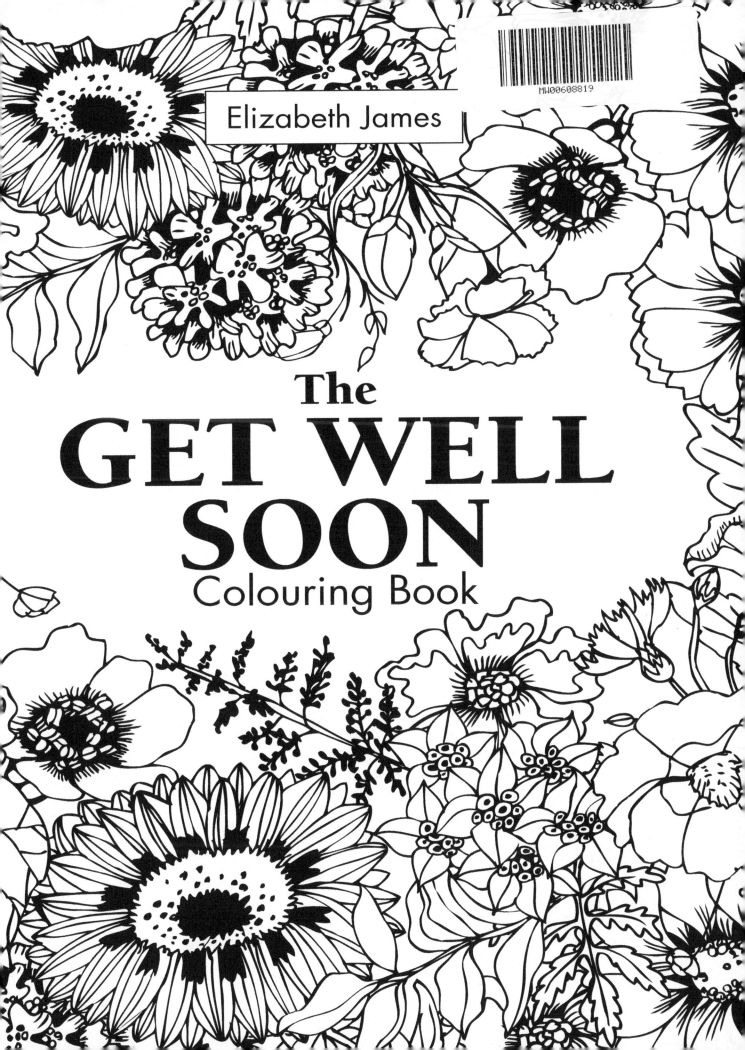

Elizabeth James

The
GET WELL
SOON
Colouring Book

First published in 2015 by Kyle Craig Publishing

Copyright © 2015 Kyle Craig Publishing

Design: Elizabeth James, Julie Anson, Alison McNicol, Shutterstock, Inc.

ISBN: 978-1-78595-089-6

A CIP record for this book is available from the British Library.

A Kyle Craig Publication

www.kyle-craig.com

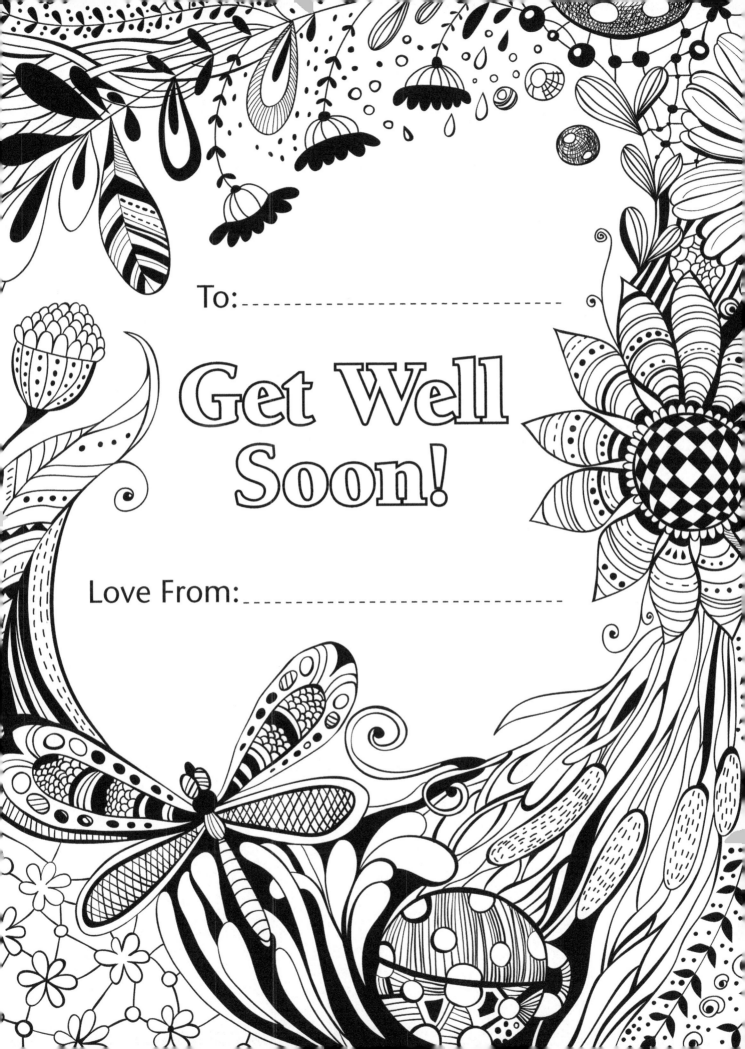

To: _____

Get Well Soon!

Love From: _____

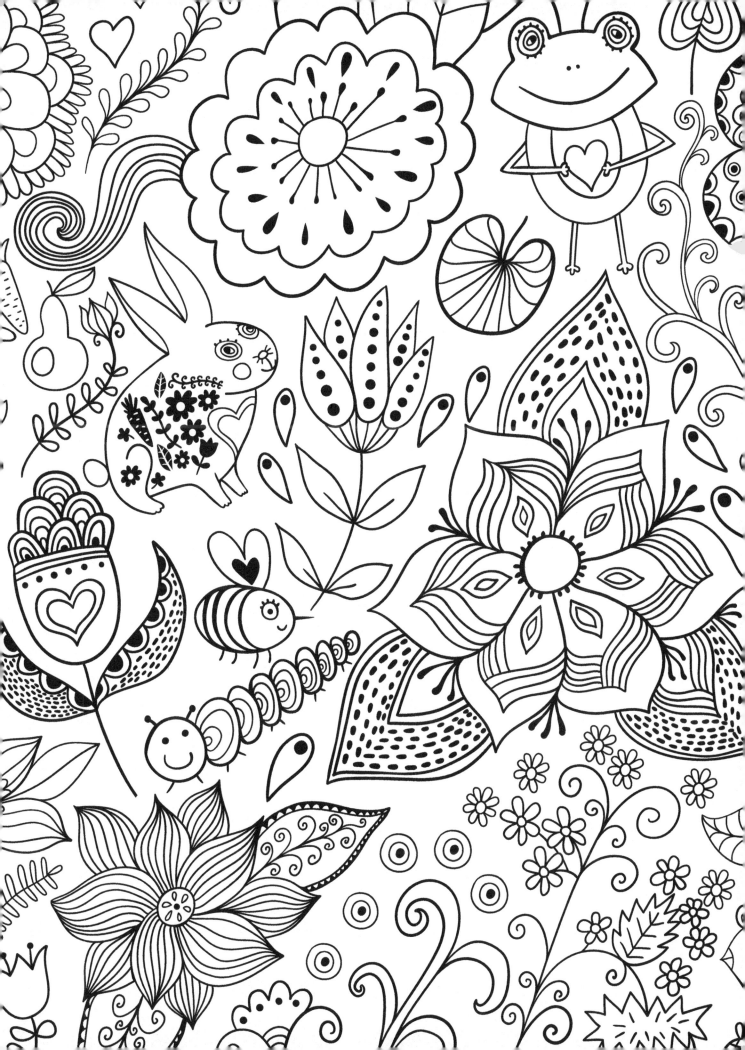

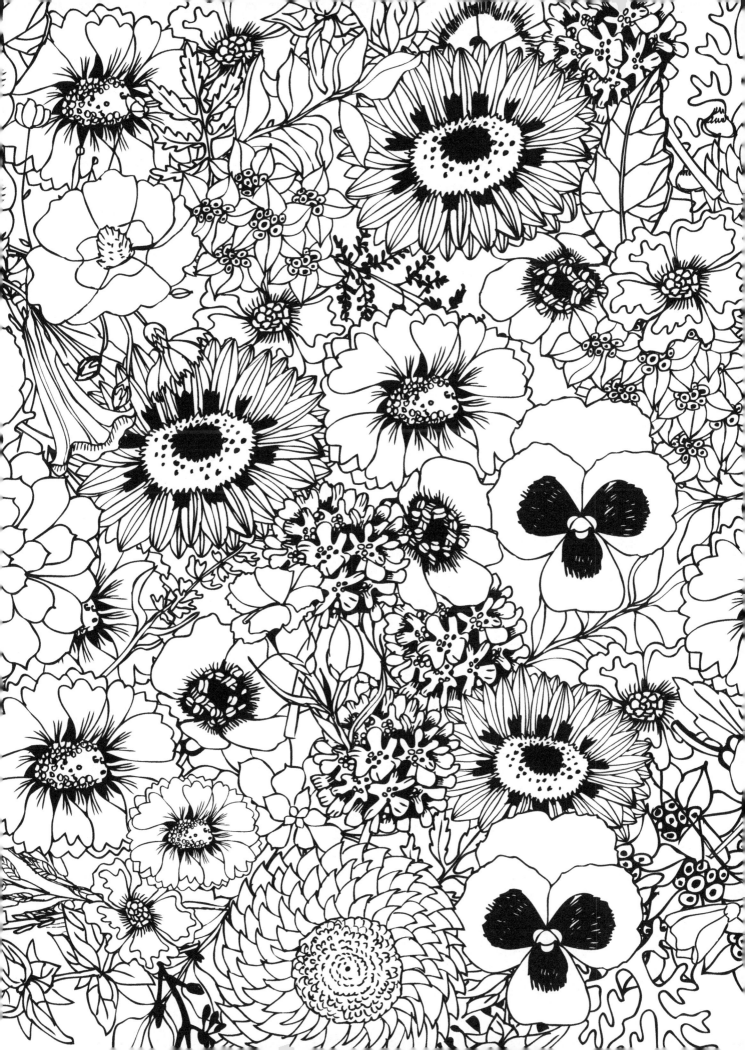

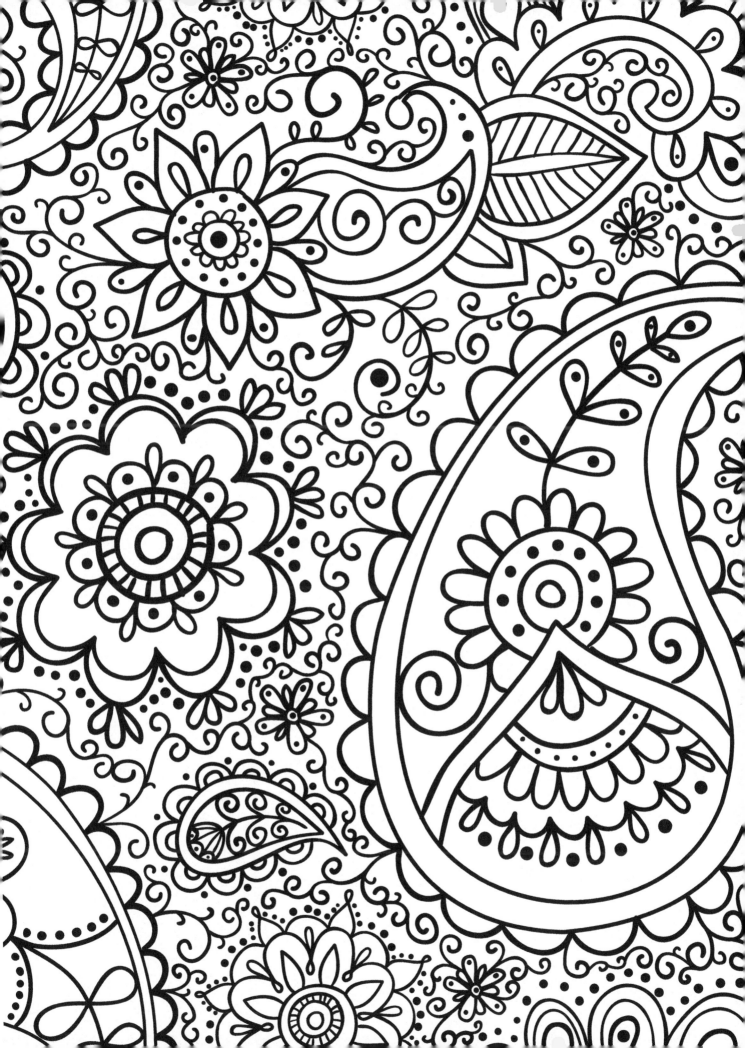

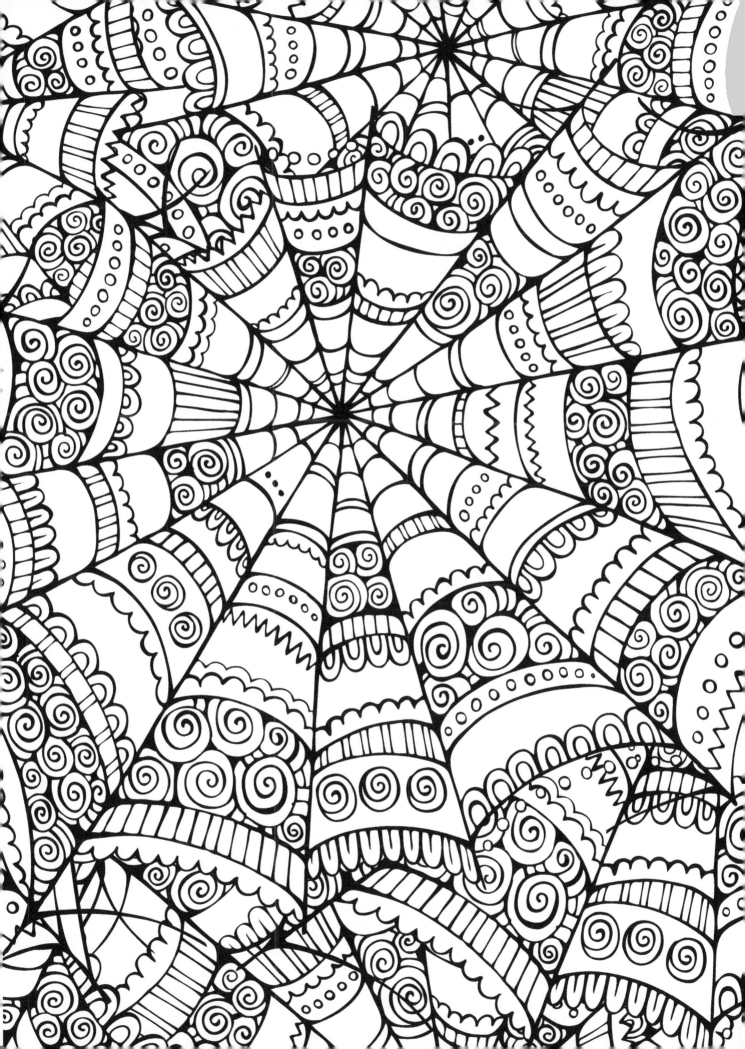

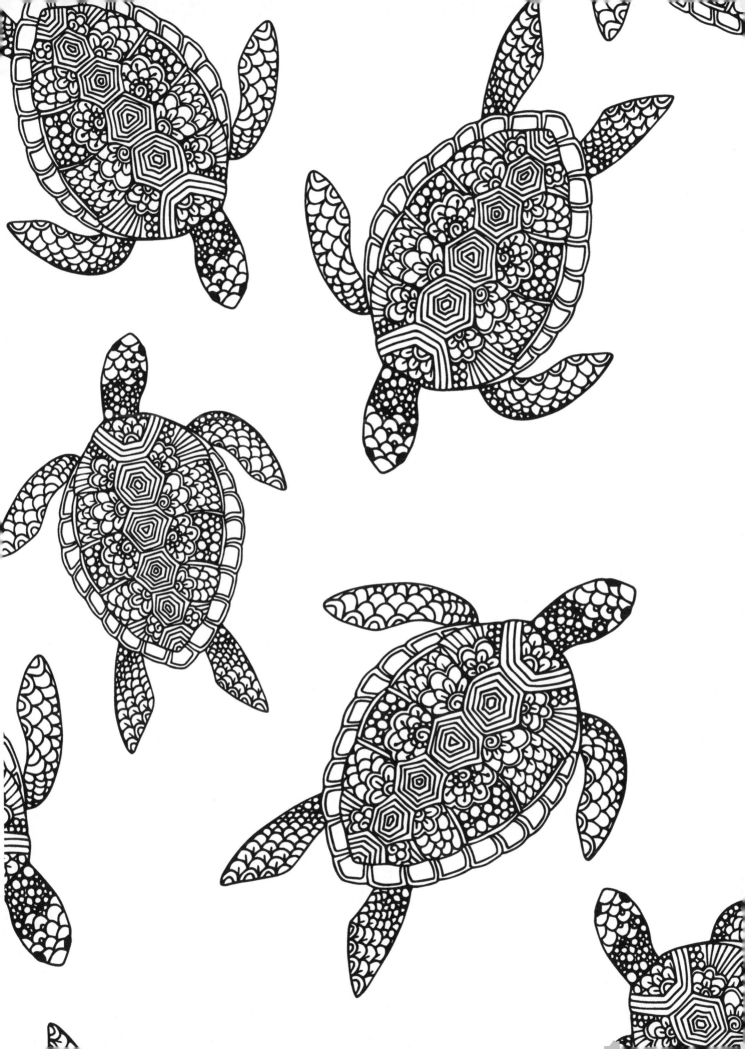

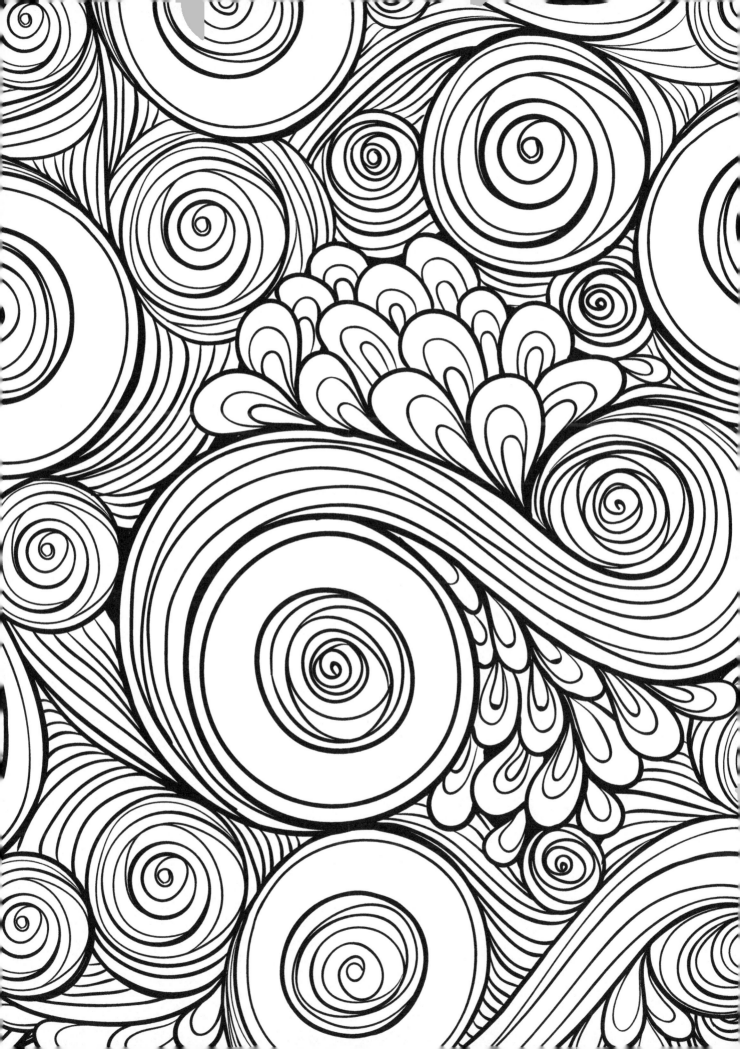

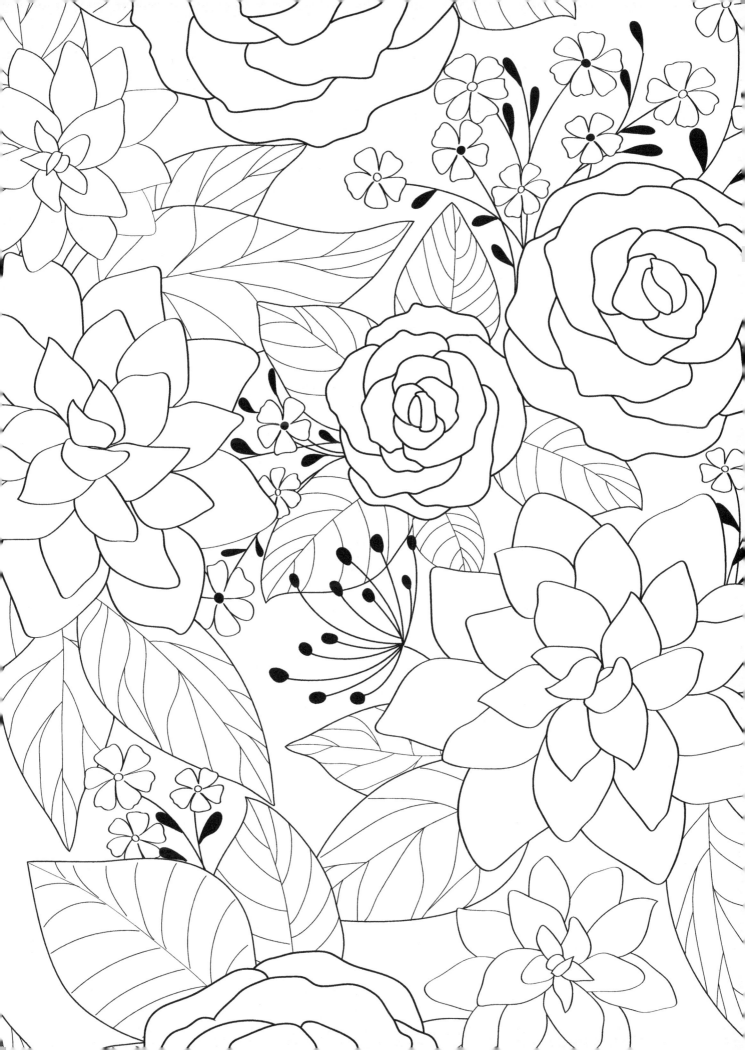

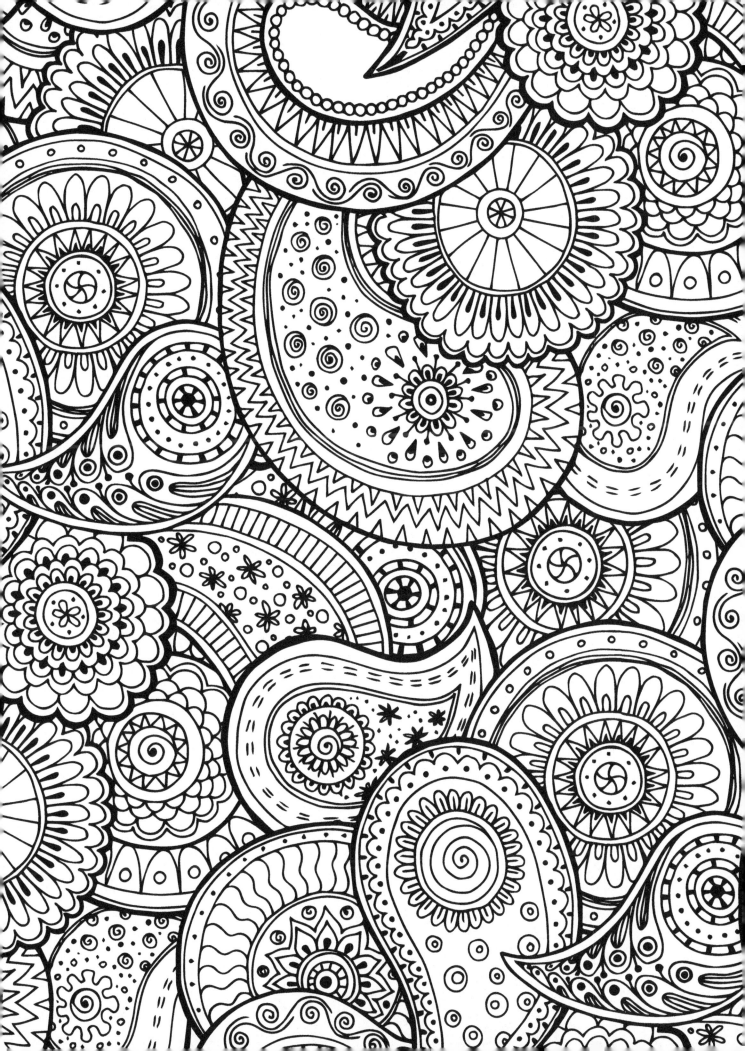

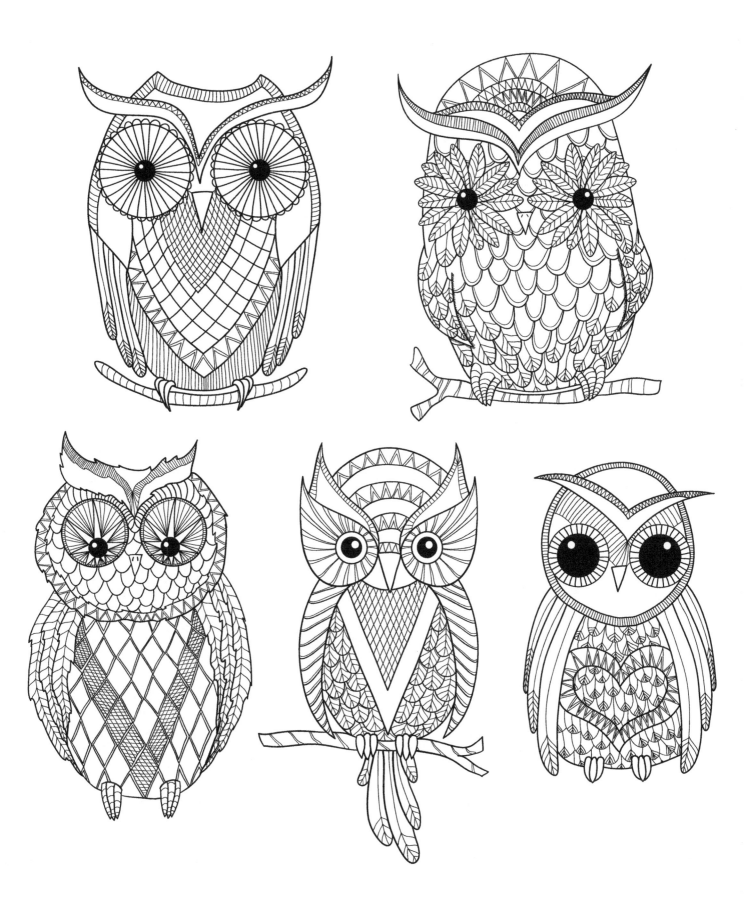

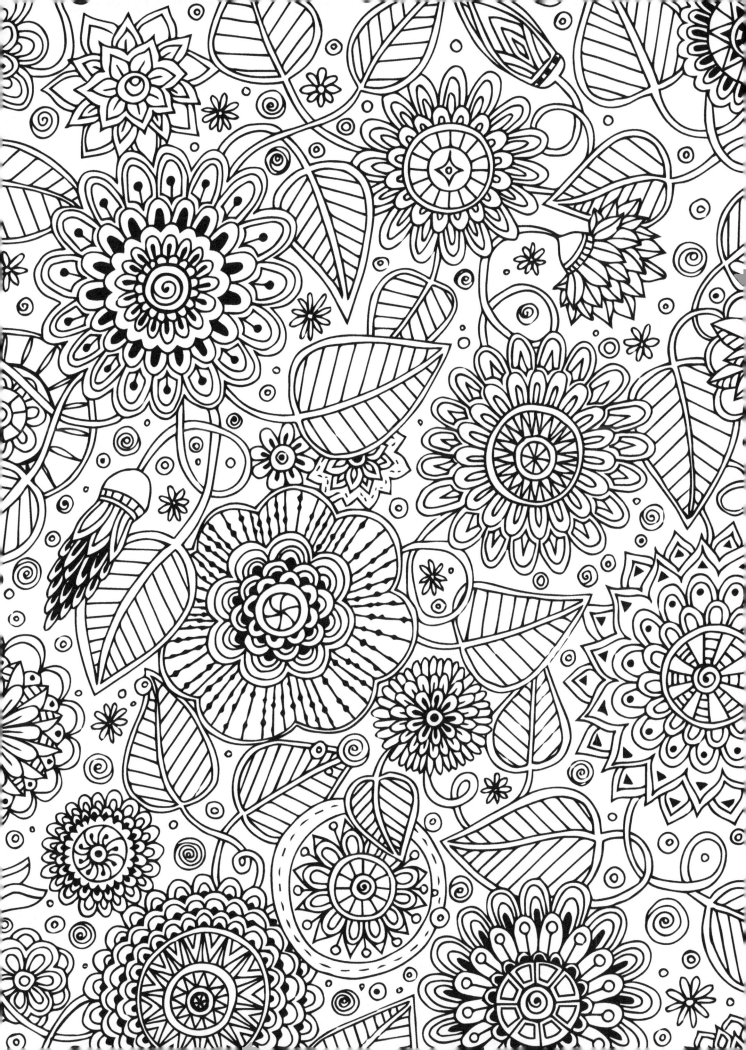

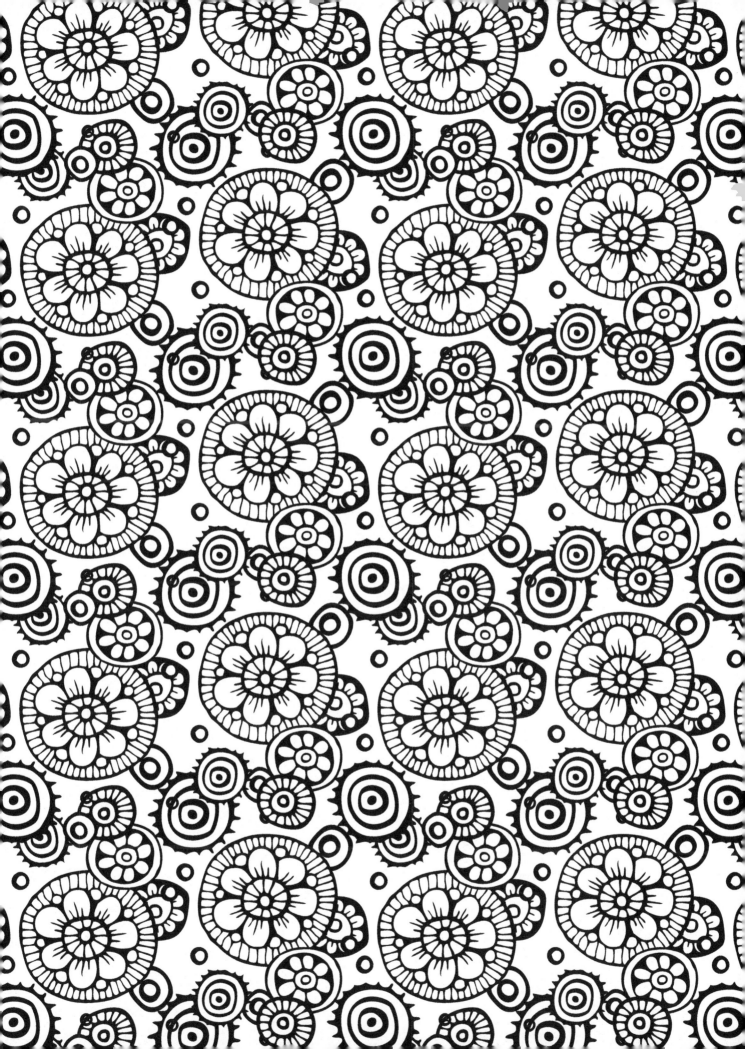

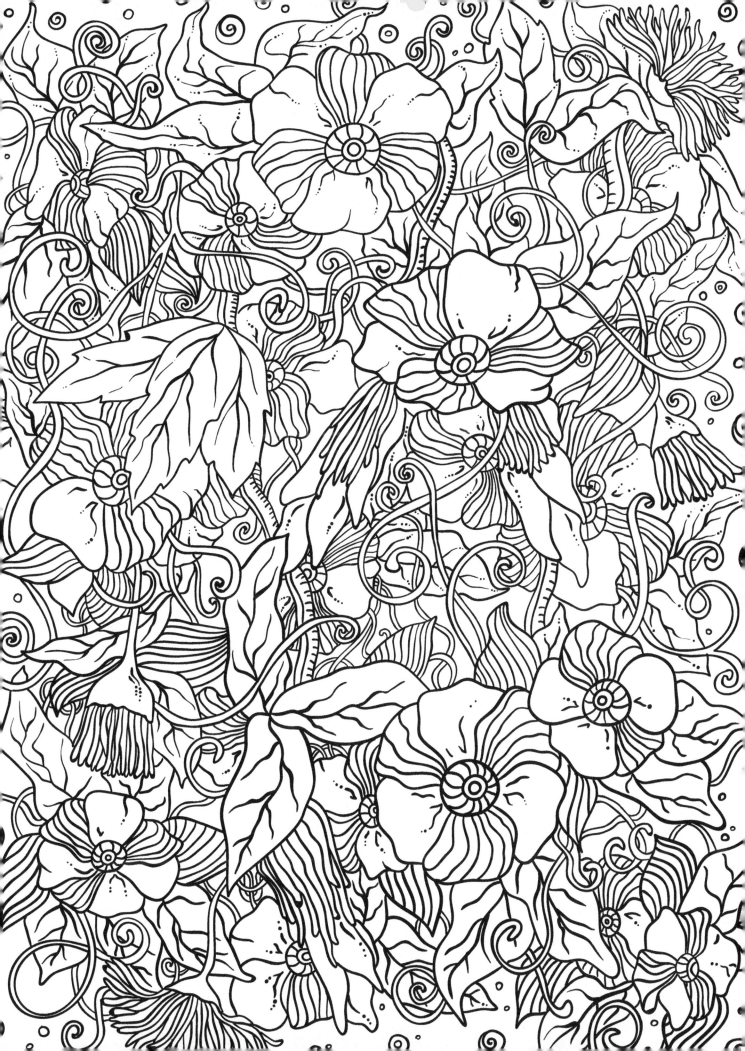

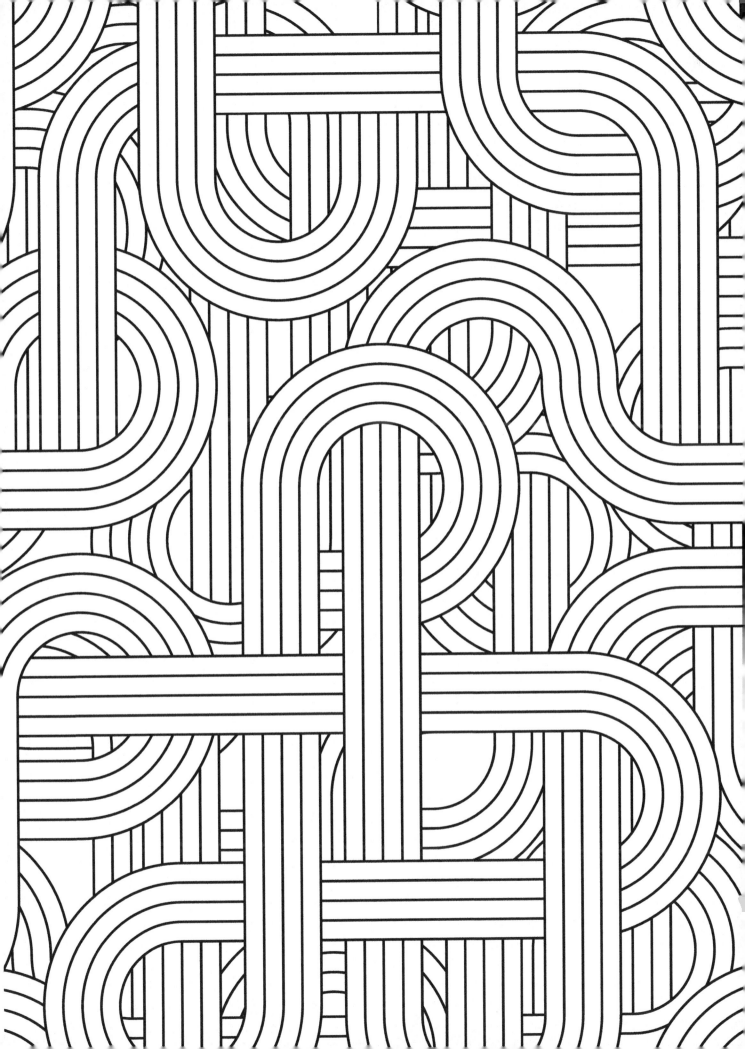

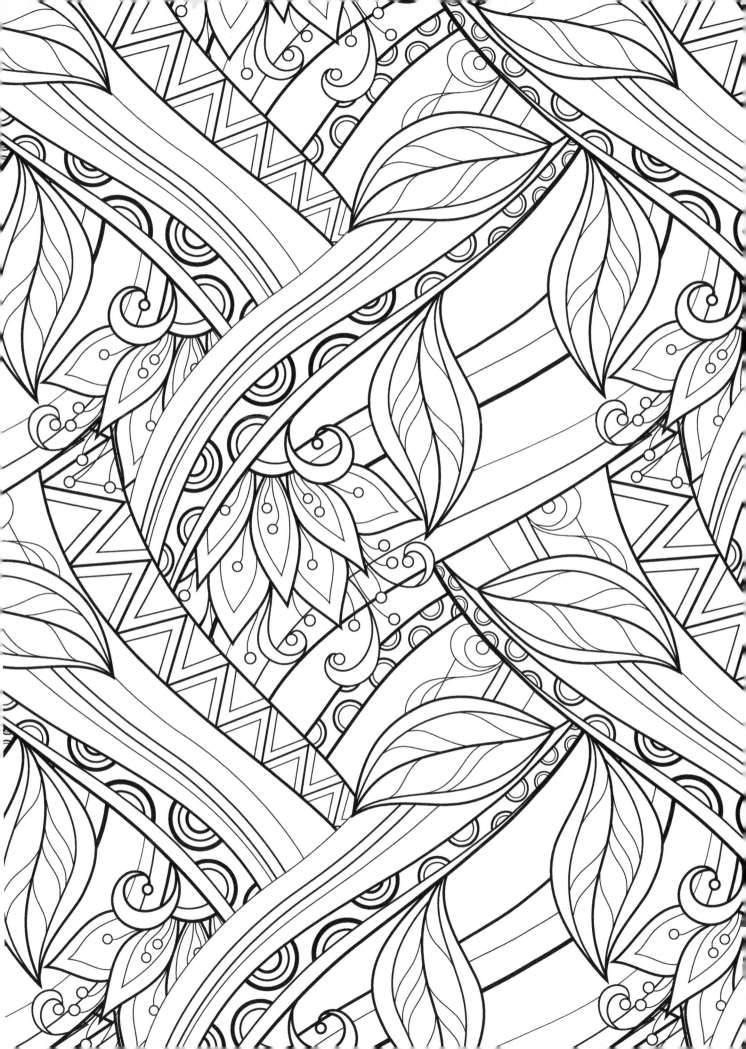

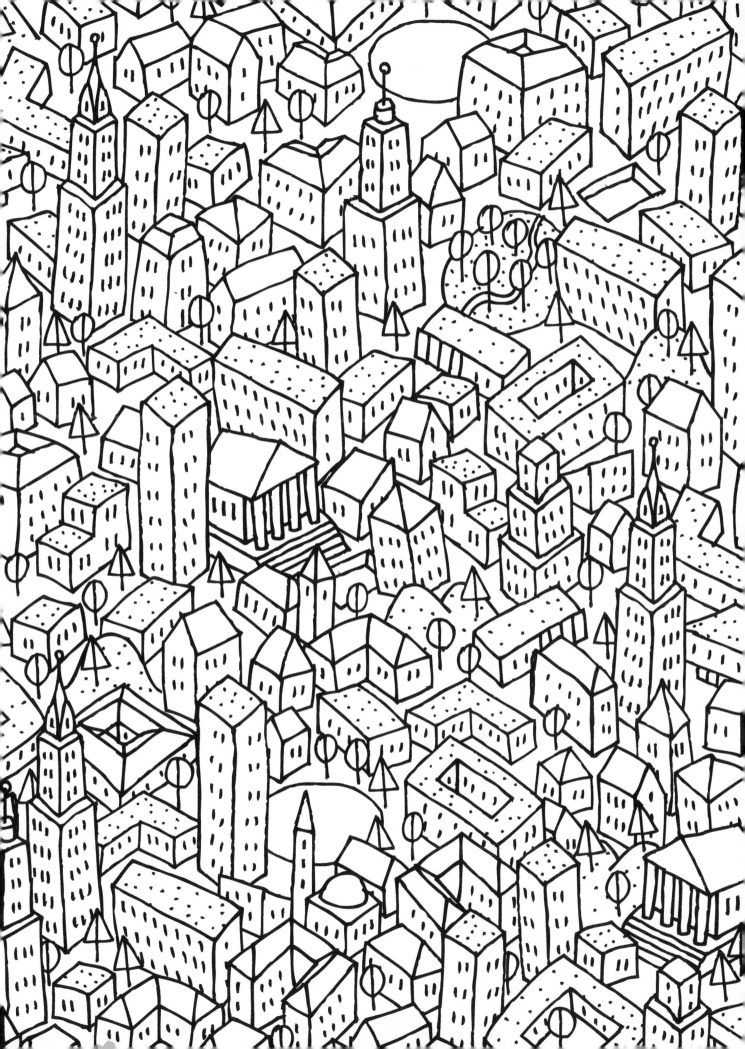

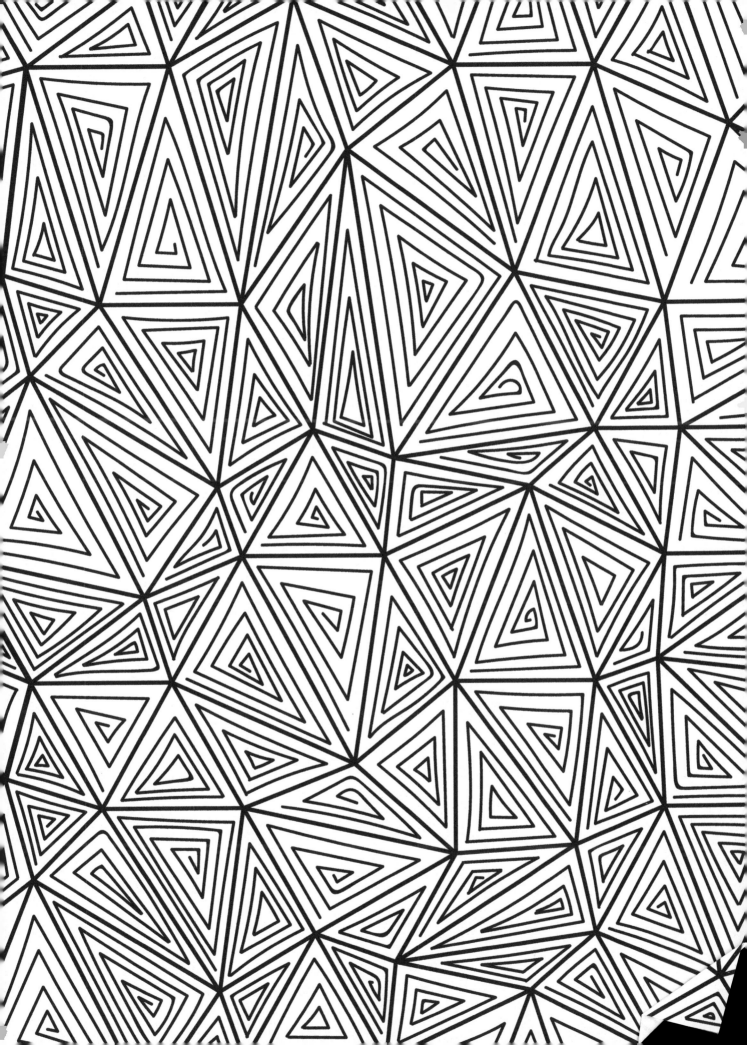

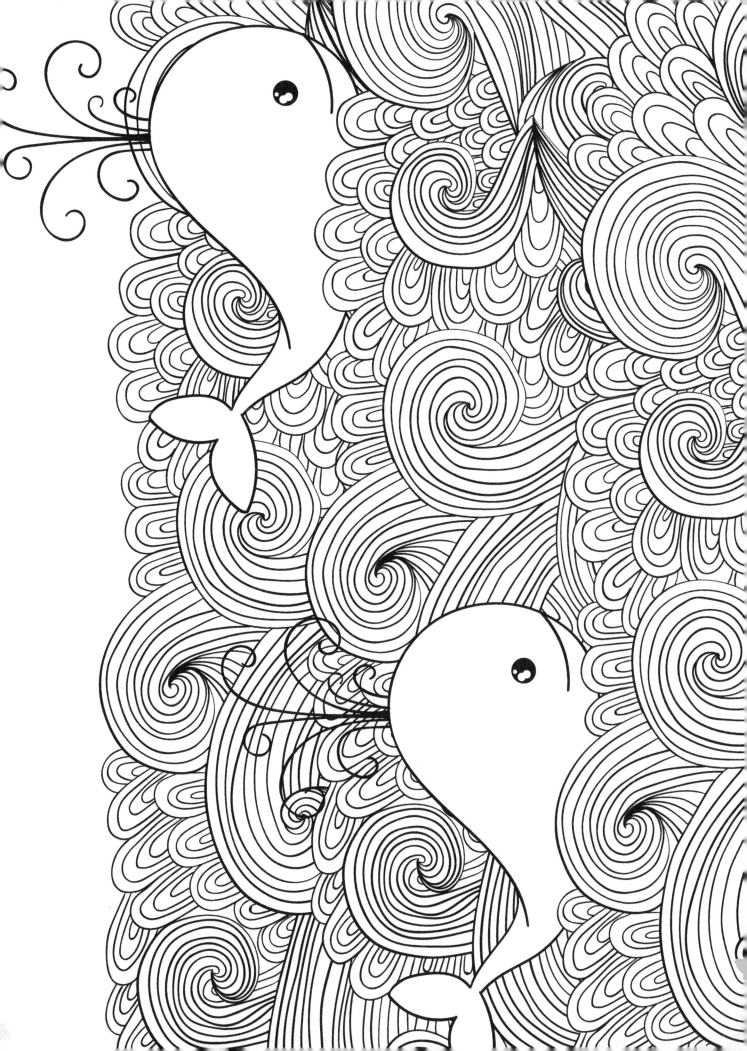

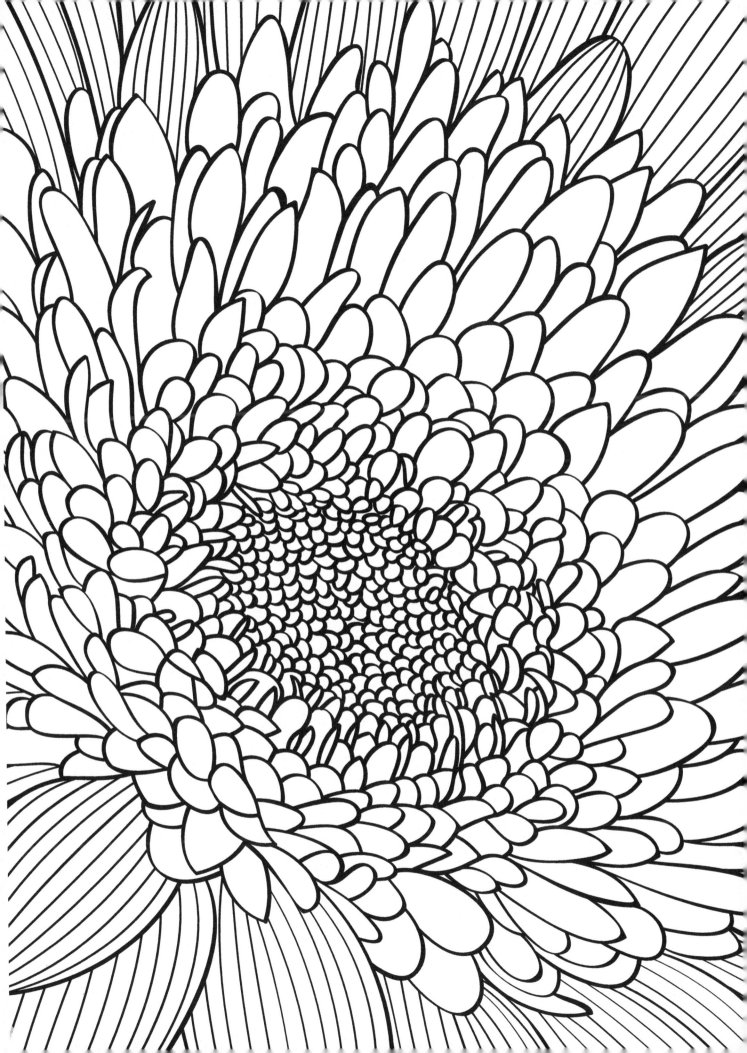

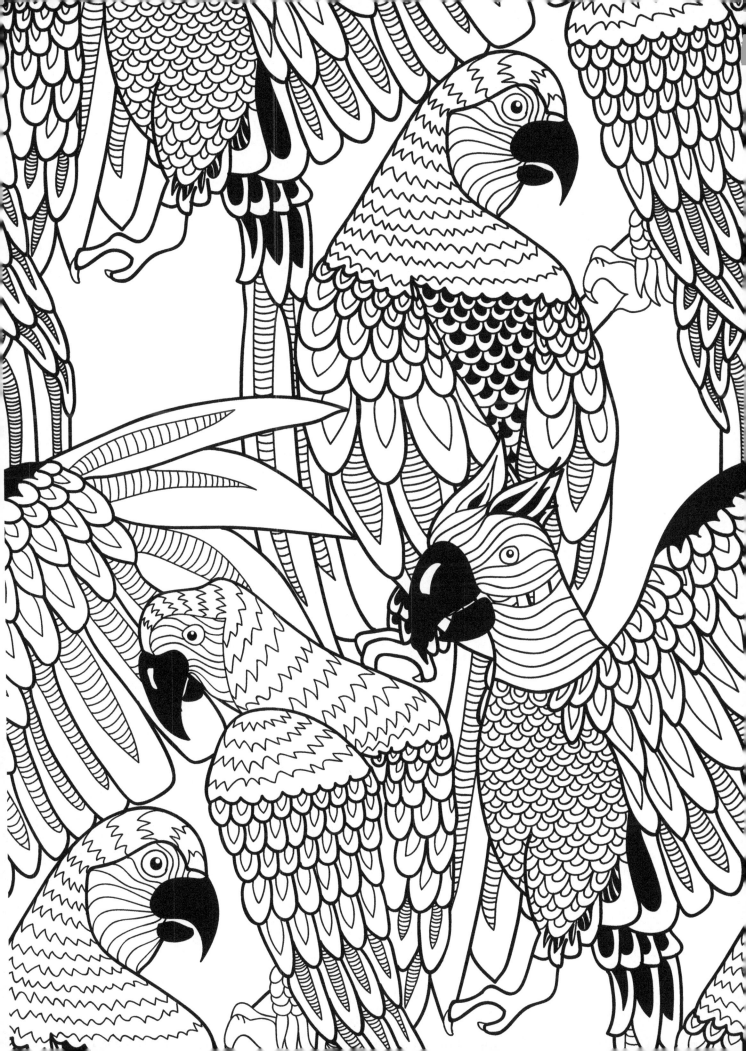

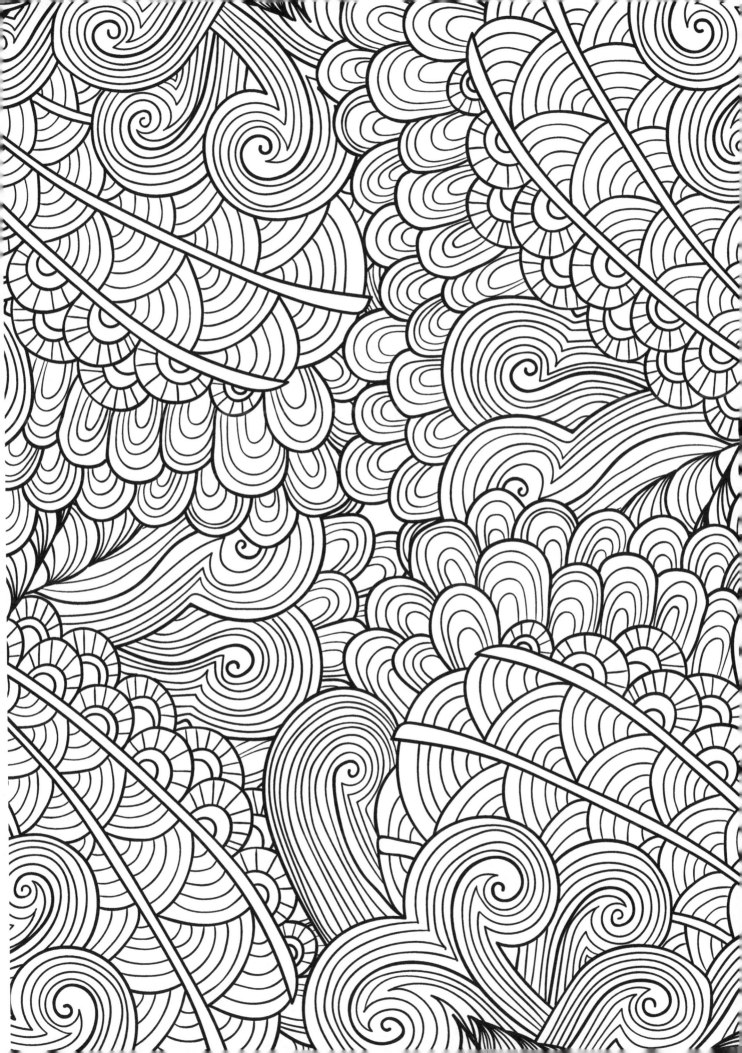

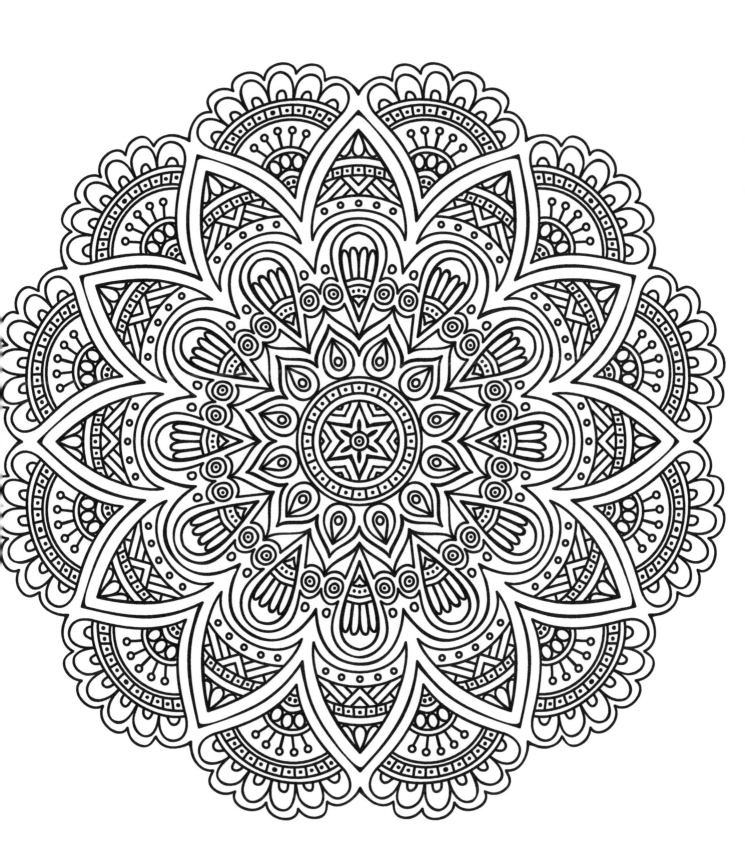

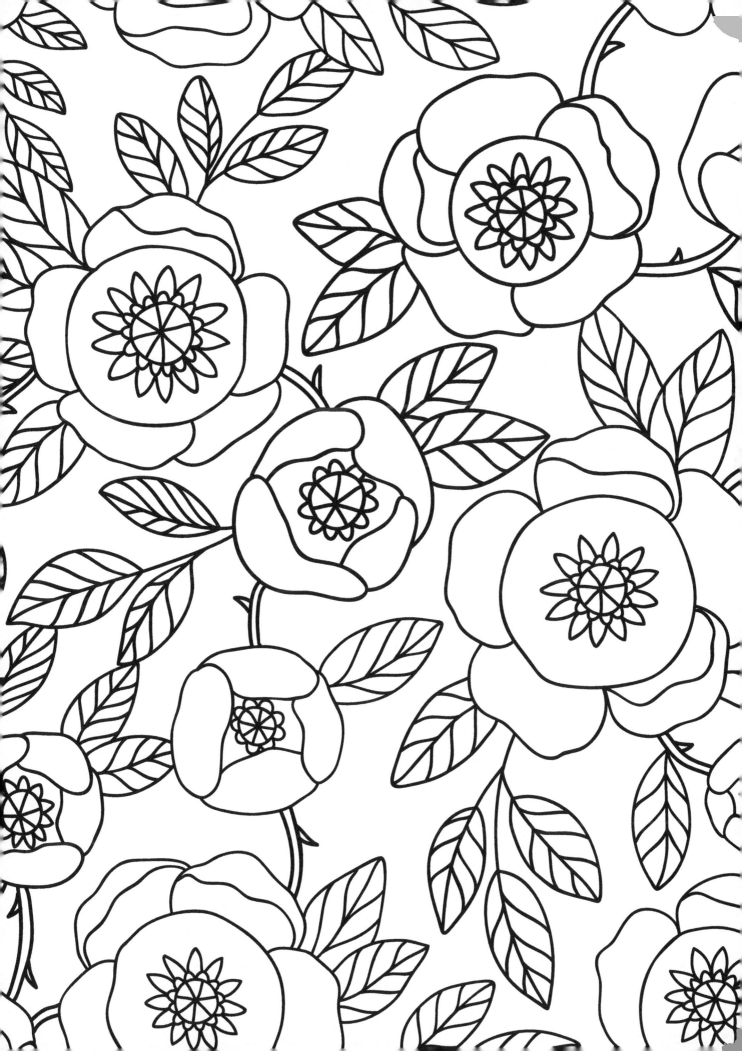

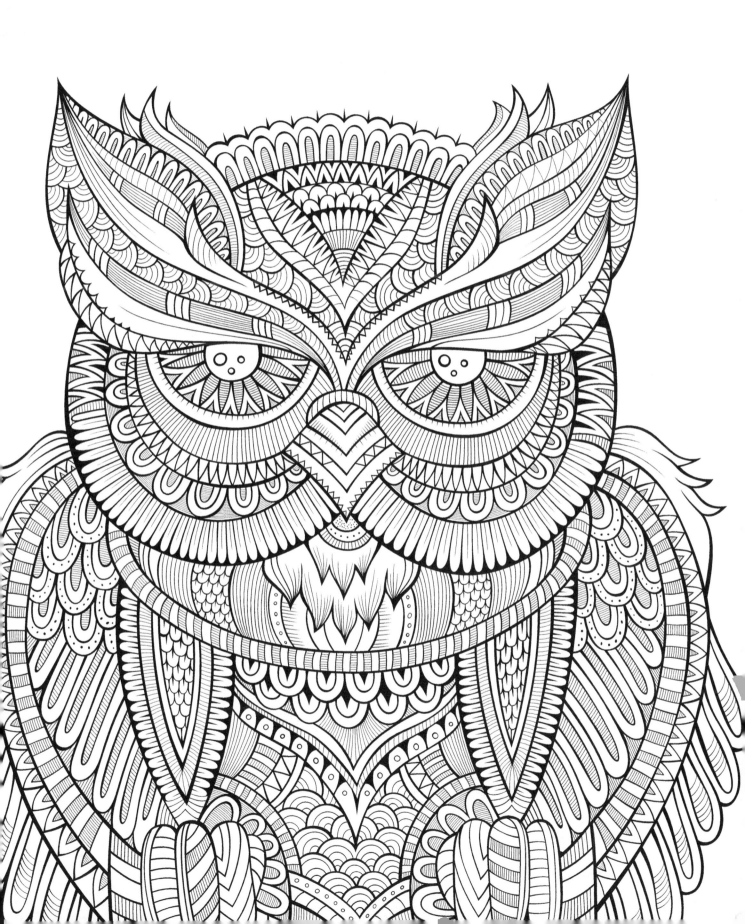

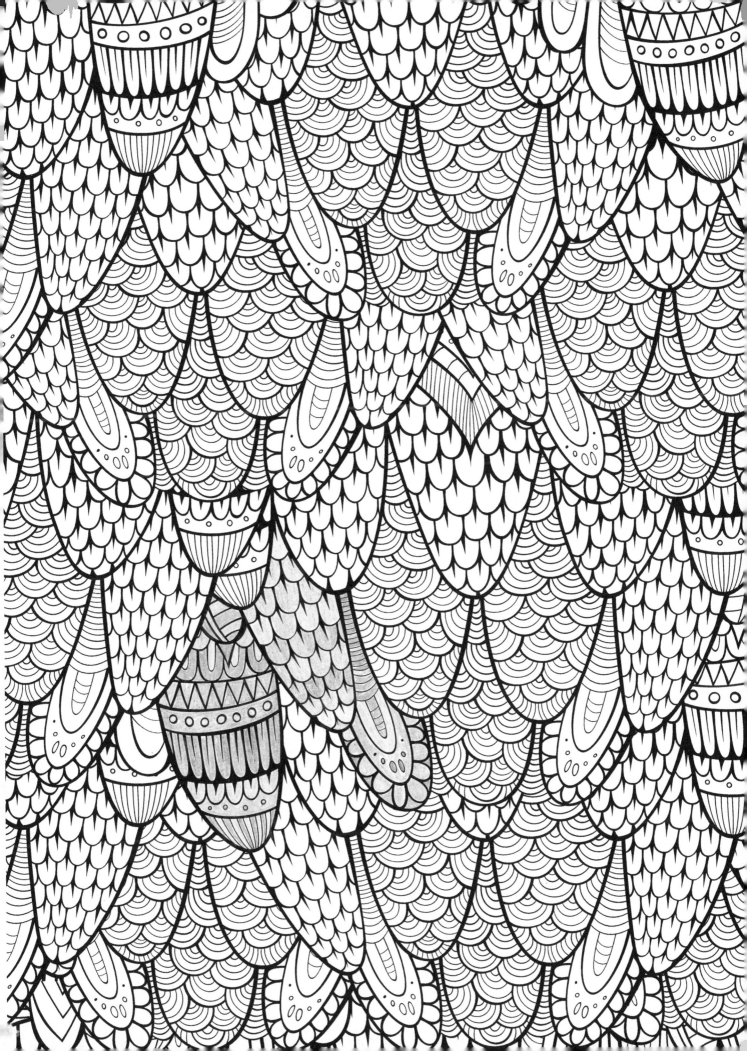

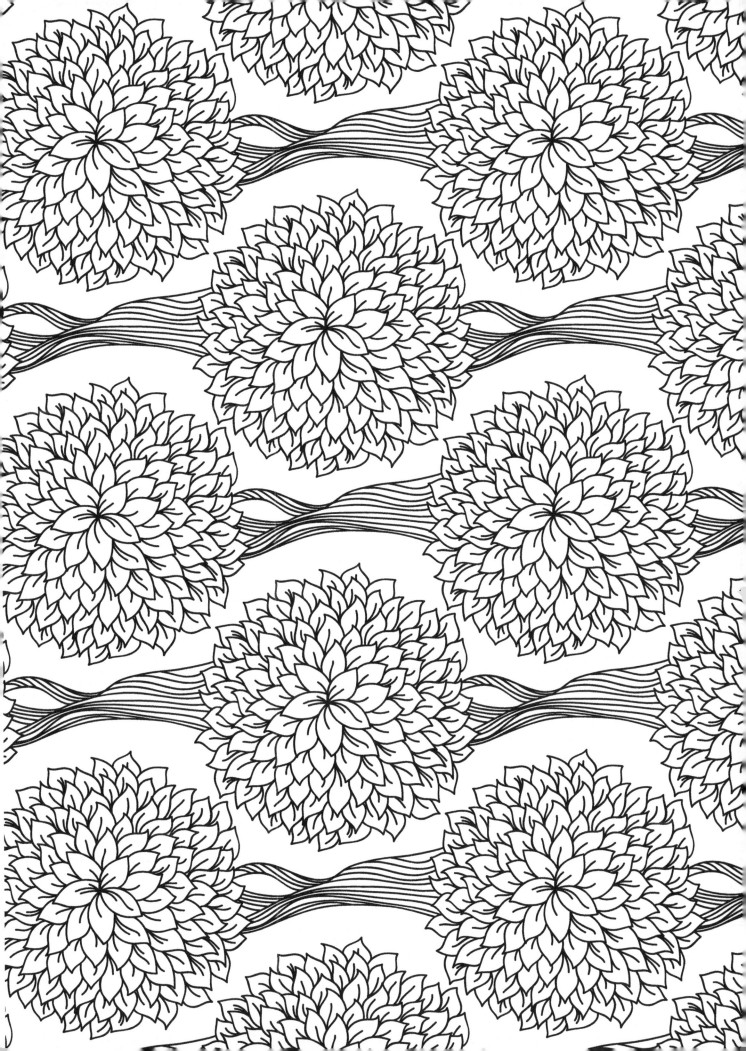

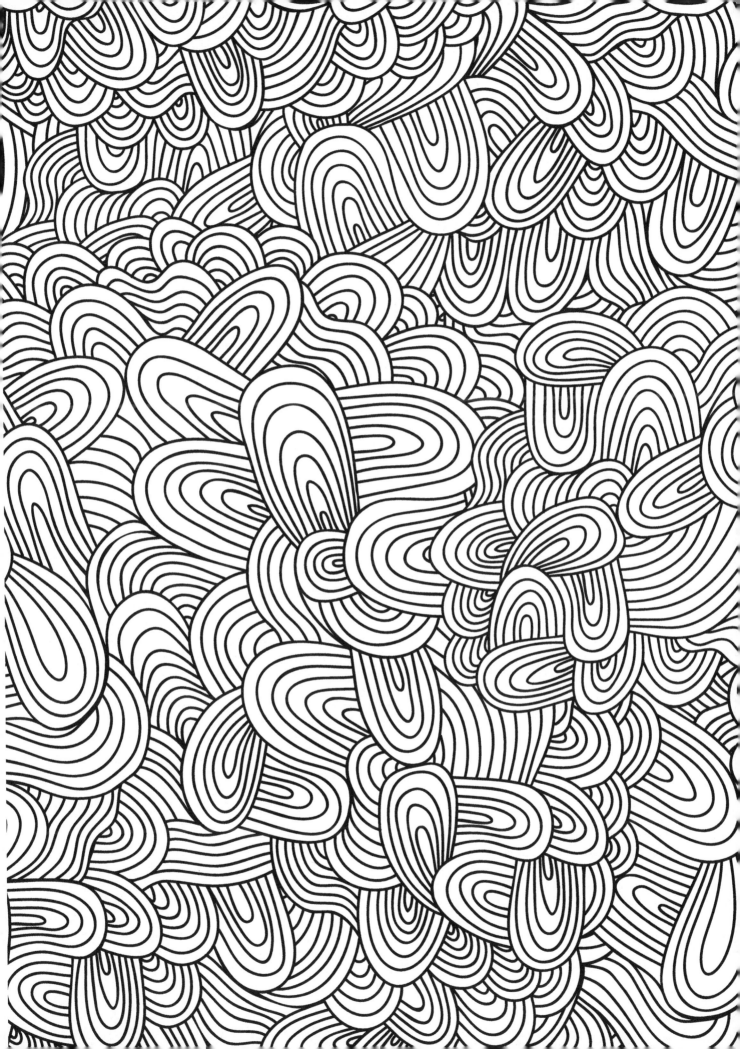

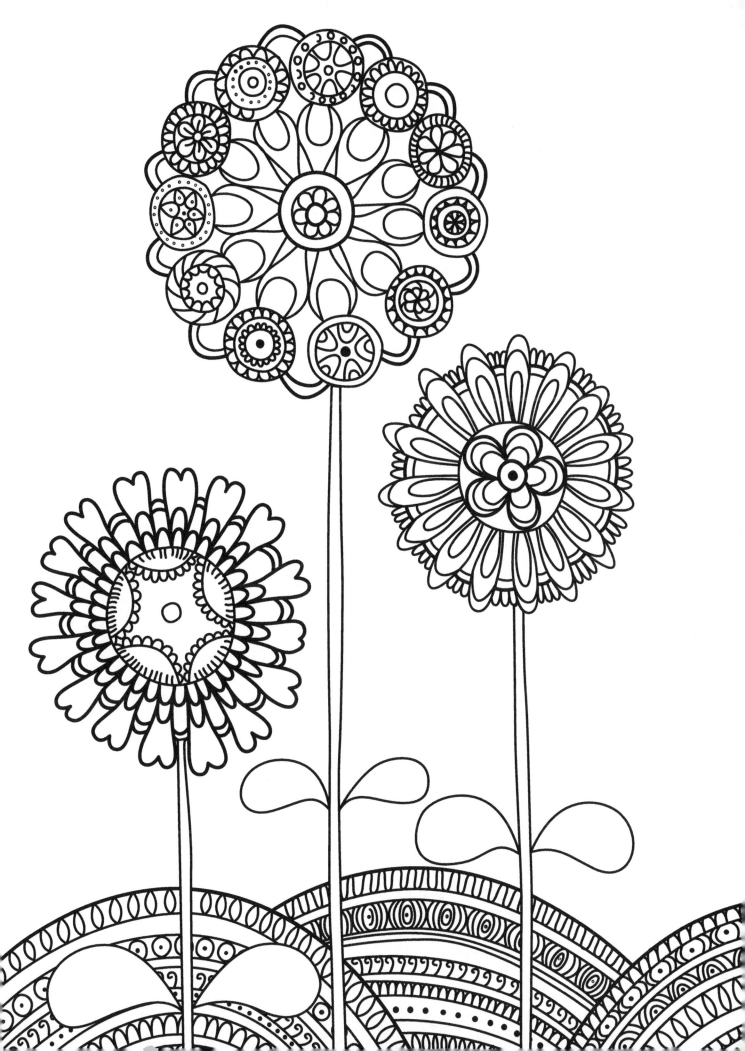